How Things Move

Fast

Sarah Shannon

Heinemann
LIBRARY

www.heinemannlibrary.co.uk
Visit our website to find out more information about Heinemann Library books.

To order:

 Phone 44 (0) 1865 888066

 Send a fax to 44 (0) 1865 314091

 Visit the Heinemann Bookshop at www.heinemannlibrary.co.uk to browse our catalogue and order online.

Heinemann Library is an imprint of Capstone Global Library Limited, a company incorporated in England and Wales having its registered office at 7 Pilgrim Street, London, EC4V 6LB – Registered company number: 6695582

Heinemann is a registered trademark of Pearson Education Limited, under licence to Capstone Global Library Limited

Edited by Siân Smith, Rebecca Rissman, and Charlotte Guillain
Designed by Joanna Hinton-Malivoire
Picture research by Elizabeth Alexander
Production by Duncan Gilbert
Originated by Dot Gradations Ltd
Printed and bound in China by South China Printing Company Ltd

ISBN 978 0 431 19322 9
13 12 11 10 09
10 9 8 7 6 5 4 3 2 1

British Library Cataloguing in Publication Data
Shannon, Sarah
   Fast. - (How things move)
   1. Speed - Juvenile literature
   I. Title
   531.1'12

Acknowledgements
We would like to thank the following for permission to reproduce photographs: ©Alamy pp.**12** (Alain Le Garsmeur), **11** (Andrea Bricco/ Brand X), **5** (Andy Newman/ epa), **8** (David LeBon/Transtock), **19** (David Spurdens), **7** (G. Bowater), **13** (Juice Images), **9** (Kevin Dodge), **4** (Lester Lefkowitz), **10** (Steve Prezant), **20** (Tom Brakefield), **14** (Wally McNamee); ©Getty Images. p.**17 right** (Gallo Images/Martin Harvey); ©iStockphoto. com pp.**6** (Kseniya Abramova), **17 left** (Heather Down); ©Photolibrary pp.**18** (Wolfgang Weinhäupl/Mauritius), **21** (Mauritius), **16** (Nonstock/ Fabrik-Studios Ltd), **15** (Stockbyte/Photodisc)

Cover photograph of a yellow car reproduced with permission of ©Corbis (David Madison). Back cover photograph of a waterskier reproduced with permission of ©Photolibrary (Stockbyte/Photodisc).

Every effort has been made to contact copyright holders of material reproduced in this book. Any omissions will be rectified in subsequent printings if notice is given to the publishers.

Contents

Moving

Things can move in many ways.

Things can move from place to place.

Moving fast

Some things can move fast.

Things that move fast take a short
time to move from place to place.

A car can move fast.

When you run, you move fast.

Pushes

A push can make something move fast.

When you push a swing it moves fast.

Pulls

A pull can make something move fast.

When you pull a sledge it moves fast.

Moving faster

When you give something a big push, it moves faster.

When you give something a big pull,
it moves faster.

A car is faster than a bicycle.

A cheetah is faster than a slug.

As something speeds up, it gets faster and faster.

As an aeroplane speeds up, it gets faster and faster.

Fast things

Lots of things can move fast.

How fast can you move?

What have you learned?

- Fast things take a short time to move from place to place.

- Pushes and pulls can make things move fast.

- A big push can make something move faster.

- A big pull can make something move faster.

Picture glossary

pull make something move towards you

push make something move away from you

Index

Notes for parents and teachers
Before reading
Talk to children about different ways to move. Sometimes we move fast and sometimes we move slowly. Ask the children for examples of when they move fast (playing football, running races, riding a bike) or slowly (in a crowded shop, waiting in line). What things can they think of that move very fast? Make a list on the board.

After reading
• Let the children roll toy cars down a ramp. Which car goes the furthest? Which car goes the quickest? Make the ramp steeper. Will the cars go quicker or slower? Why?
• Read the children the traditional tale *The Gingerbread Man*. Teach them the refrain: "Run, run as fast as you can. You can't catch me, I'm a gingerbread man."
• In the hall challenge the children to move as fast (and as safely!) as they can. Then to move as slowly as they can.
• Tell the children to look through magazines and catalogues. They should cut out pictures of things that move fast. Then they should agree which things go the fastest. Stick these on a large length of card in order of speed.

PILLGWENLLY

26-07-18